IMAGES OF ENGLAND

# Buntingford

River Green Bridge, c. 1923. In 1852, the Layston Vestry decided to build a carriage bridge over the River Rib at River Green. Mr. Charles Gray's tender of £95 was accepted but, as he did not keep to specification, he had £2 deducted from his fee. The bridge was completed by October, 1852. In 1994, the bridge was rebuilt having earlier had wooden shoring installed under the arch. River Green is mentioned in the 1622 Sessions Rolls.

IMAGES OF ENGLAND

# Buntingford

Philip W. Plumb

NONSUCH

Silver Jubilee, 1977. Prince George of Denmark presents a cup to Eddie Plume. Charlie Edwards on the left, then Princess Anne of Denmark, Roma Greensmith, and Valierie Hobson (Mrs John Profumo).

First published 1995
This new pocket edition 2005
Images unchanged from first edition

Nonsuch Publishing Limited
The Mill, Brimscombe Port,
Stroud, Gloucestershire, GL5 2QG
www.nonsuch-publishing.com

British Library Cataloguing in Publication Data.
A catalogue record for this book is available from the British Library.

ISBN 1-84588-133-8

Typesetting and origination by Nonsuch Publishing Limited
Printed in Great Britain by Oaklands Book Services Limited

# Contents

Acknowledgements     6

Introduction     7

1.     The Heart of Buntingford     9

2.     Church and School     23

3.     Houses and Other Buildings     35

4.     At Your Service!     49

5.     Sporting Activities     57

6.     Recreation and Leisure     67

7.     Trade and Industry     77

8.     Places of Refreshment     97

9.     Occasions and People     103

10.     Buntingford at War     111

11.     Round the District     121

# Acknowledgements

Many people have contributed to this book by giving or lending photographs to be copied or by identifying those who appear in the pictures. These include Stanley Attwood, Frank Aylott, Joan Bailey, Lavinia Baker, Vera Bishop, Myrtle and Eric Brownless, Doris Budgen, Phyllis Cornes, Sylvia Downham, Bernard Edwards, Madge and Stan Glazebrook, Tom Gray, Ian Jefferies (who has built up a Civic Society collection of photos), David Mander, Nancy and David Mayes, Derrick Muggleton, Bob Piggott, Jenny and John Reynolds, Dick Rye, Joan Scholes, Gordon Sibthorpe, Byron Smith, Elsie Smith, Ray Staniland, Bert Thody, Michael Thody, Ruth Thody, Cecil Tottman, Stanley Waters, Eunice and Chris Woods. The following organisations have kindly allowed material in their keeping to be reproduced: Buntingford Library, East Herts Archaeological Society, Hertfordshire Local Studies Library, Hertfordshire Record Office, Natwest Group Archives. Special thanks are due to Peter Knight, Churchills, Chartered Surveyors, Buntingford, who readily agreed to sponsor this book. I am grateful to Dulcie, Jenny and Martin Plumb for help in checking the proofs.

# Introduction

Over many years I have been collecting photographs of Buntingford and its immediate vicinity. To those handed down by my parents (my late mother was particularly helpful in locating and identifying photos, people and incidents), I have added postcards and other pictures from many sources. Friends have lent their precious photos for copying. Also I have been given some small but significant collections which are well represented in this book. These are from the late Stan Attwood and the late Stanley Waters. Acknowledgements to others will be found opposite.

This is a book which is both too soon and too late. Too soon because there are many interesting and significant photos of Buntingford still to be revealed. Some surfaced even during the time that copy was being sent to the publishers. The book is too late because so many of those, including my own parents, who would have enjoyed the memories aroused by seeing again people and incidents from the past, are no longer with us.

No Buntingford names are listed in trade directories under the category of photographer. However, there were men (no women, I think) who were photographers, at least semi-professionally, and produced expert prints, mounted, with their names printed underneath or on the photo itself. These were Albert Frederick Bishop, Albert George Bishop, John Bishop, Jack Bishop, A.H. Howard, W. Leatham Sworder, and H. Clarke, Two years ago, a collector of glass negatives, Byron Smith, of Welwyn Garden City, purchased a collection which proved to be largely, if not entirely, taken by Harry A. Jackson, butcher, of High Street, Buntingford. The Jackson and Handy families were related and so many shots concern the latter, including the building of St. Richard's Church. Some of the pictures of the unveiling of the Scouts' shrine (see page 112) were issued as postcards with Jackson's name and address printed over them. The Royston photographer, Robert H. Clark produced many cards of Buntingford. The various stationers and newsagents frequently published their own series but without naming the photographer: E.E. Darville, A.G .Day, J. May. H. Clarke also took cine films which were very popular with the local audiences. He also sold wirelesses and as he was manager of the local labour exchange he led a busy life. Some cards appear with Gilbert and Clarke on and one with W.A. Gilbert, Buntingford.

Dating is not always as simple as with those pictures which are of named events such as royal weddings and funerals. The huge and obtrusive telegraph poles in the High Street were erected just before May 1907. Postmarks must be used with caution as although, of course, the photographs cannot date from after the postmark, they may have been taken many years earlier, One card postmarked 1917 is clearly pre-poles. Sometimes dates have been assigned by previous owners which are certainly wrong.

Names are most important but are not always available, or in the case of groups, only some are known. We must be grateful to those photographers who printed all the names on the bottom and to those townspeople who, many years after the event, sent an old picture to a local newspaper and identified those appearing. It is intended that this selection will give a portrait of Buntingford conveying something of its charm, which still exists despite the many changes over the years. Physically, the town has changed very markedly. Of the many large houses with gardens which existed until after the Second World War in the town itself, only one remains. The green spaces such as Porter's Close and the Football Ground have been built over. The loss of the latter was a serious blow to the town's amenities and the Club has not yet recovered from its loss and consequent homelessness. On the positive side there are now public gardens and a community centre.

The choice of shops, as in most similar communities, is now much restricted and the loss of the railway and the cinema reflect the experience of many larger towns. The schools, however, play an important role in the town and achieve standards which give much hope for the future. There is much interest in our past but the inevitability of so many of the students leaving Buntingford for higher education and then a career diminishes the stock of those able and willing to shoulder the responsibilities borne by those portrayed in these pages.

*One*

# The Heart of Buntingford

High Street and Market Hill, *c.* 1903. Buntingford was founded as a trading centre for the surrounding manors and estates early in the twelfth century. The Market Hill and the High Street leading from it are its heart. With two public houses, a chemist's shop, a baker, a draper, post office, and a tannery, the small area shown was a miniature town in itself in the early years of this century.

High Street, c. 1830. The topographical artists, John and J.C. Buckler, made nearly one thousand monochrome drawings of Hertfordshire between 1809 and 1845, and these form an invaluable record of the county. They are housed in the County Record Office, Hertford. The High Street had a very Medieval appearance then and many of these buildings have vanished over the 150 years since this view.

High Street c. 1903, looking south. The George and Dragon Hotel is on the left and further down is another baker's shop, now a green grocer's, from which the small charity loaves were distributed annually. On the right is the canopy of one of the several butchers' shops then trading in the town.

High Street *c.* 1912, looking north. The telegraph poles erected in 1907 are prominent as are the traces of passing horses being cleared away to be used as manure. The house on the right with a butcher's shop next door was at one time the police station and had a secure prison cell at the back with iron bars above the double boarded door. The shop front has been replaced by a domestic façade. The magnificent horse chestnut has been felled

High Street *c.* 1912, looking south. St. Peter's Chapel of Ease can be seen at the end of the High street. On the left the mixture of flag stones and cobbles shows the surface of the pavement. A cart stands outside the grocer's shop, one of the Feasey stores, later Forrest's Stores.

High Street *c.* 1903, looking north. By this date, the George and Dragon Hotel was the principal inn in the town. To the right is Hamilton's, the ironmongers. Part of the dress-making shop run by Mrs Annie Stapley is seen on the left: this was also the Layston Laundry managed by her husband Alfred. Next is F. Feasey's grocery.

High Street *c.* 1904, looking south. On the right is the Globe public house with two signs advertising cycles and motor repairs.

High Street c. 1920, looking north. On the left is the shop of A.G. Day, newsagent, stationer and bookseller, publisher of this postcard. Next is the Angel Inn and between them the archway over which is the town clock, all owned by the Buntingford Charity trustees. On the other side of the road is a cycle shop.

Royston Road, c. 1920. At the north end of the High Street is the entrance to the Layston Vicarage drive (on the right) and beyond that is Corneybury Park.

London Road *c.* 1905, facing the town. Just past the last of the houses on the left is the road to the railway station.

London Road some 25 years later.

Sunny Hill looking into the town in the 1920s. The recently built council houses are on the right and in the distance at the foot of the hill is the Union Workhouse.

River Green in the 1920s with plenty of water in the River Rib. The large house is Layston Cottage, the residence of the last Master Tanner, Henry Ashford, after he moved from the High Street.

Station Road, c. 1920. On the left is the thatched public house, the Adam and Eve, now demolished and replaced by a petrol station. One sign showing Adam and Eve naked aroused adverse comment from some of the more conventional residents.

New Town, c. 1912. Paddock Road and Garden Road were known as New Town. Paddock Road, shown here, was the scene of the murder of a small boy on his way to school in 1911. A woman ran up to him and cut his throat. She had some years before thrown another small boy in to the Rib but he was rescued. For the first crime she served a few months in prison but for the murder she was found insane

High Street, *c.* 1906. Although postmarked 1917, the card shows the town before the erection of the telegraph posts

High Street, 1910. The building on the left with the gas lamp was the Bell Inn but had by now ceased to be a licensed house. Just to the left of the first telegraph post is the Carpenter's Arms which became a harness maker's shop about this time.

Market Hill c. 1903, looking north. One wing of the Almshouses is on the left, then comes the Crown Public House, the Telephone Exchange, the Manor House (standing back) and then the bank and various shops.

Market Hill, c. 1920. A similar view with the trees more mature and the ubiquitous telegraph poles intruding. The market had been in abeyance for over a century when it was decided to revive it in 1920. A weekly auction market had been started in May 1920 and a year later the new market was officially inaugurated based on the 1542 Charter. G. Scarborough Taylor was granted a seven year lease to run it.

Market day, 1923. The pens for cattle and sheep can be seen under the trees. There is an interesting variety of transport. On the right is The Manse, earlier in the century the residence of the Rev. George F. Elliott, Congregational Minister. The building became a shop in the 1930s.

Market Day, 1928. The auctioning of cattle is being done amongst great interest from buyers and onlookers. In the background are the Master Tanner's House, also at one time named Cheriton, and the Post Office.

Market Hill in the snow, April 24, 1908.

Fire destroys the Epicure Delicatessen, 1974. Formerly a sweet shop run by Miss Ethel Morgan, sister of the first catholic priest at St. Richard's, and then later by Mrs. Hilda Castle, the delicatessen caught fire through an electrical fault and could not be saved.

Floods, 1968. Exceptionally heavy rain caused widespread flooding throughout the district in 1968. The River Rib rose many feet above its banks and all low lying buildings along its course were flooded to a depth of several feet. The tractor was one way of getting about the town.

Layston Dairy flooded, 1968. Frank Aylott, the dairyman, is shown outside his front door while his wife Margaret and aunt Cissie look down from an upstairs window.

Market Hill, *c.* 1903. The pump in the middle of the photo provided water before the mains water supply was constructed. Henry Aylott, coal merchant and removal contractor, is in the group around the pump. His carts are being driven up the High Street.

# Two

# Church and School

Layston Church, c. 1903. The original name of the church was Leofstans Church (although the spelling varied widely) and it was built or rebuilt by the grandfather of the first Lord Mayor of London sometime before 1115. The present building dates from the thirteenth and fifteenth centuries. The roof of the nave has now been removed and the chancel made into a cemetery chapel.

*Left*: Medieval alabaster found at Layston 1953. During the work undertaken to make Layston Church weatherproof, these remains of a crucifixion made of alabaster were discovered. It is thought to date from about 1400. It is now in the care of the East Herts Archaeological Society at Hertford Museum.

*Below:*The Causeway elms, *c.* 1923. Layston Church is about half a mile from the town and is reached by the Causeway which, until the elm disease disaster, was lined by these beautiful trees.

*Opposite above*: St. Mary's Church, Aspenden, about 1906. Dating back to the eleventh century with additions and alterations throughout the years including a major interior restoration in 1883 by Sir Arthur Blomfield (who did much restoration throughout Hertfordshire in Victorian times), the church is Grade I and of outstanding interest for the SE chapel, the roofs, Easter Sepulchre and fine monuments to Sir Robert Clifford, Elizabeth Freman, Ralph and William Freman and John Boldero inside and Seth Ward's monument to his parents on the exterior.

Christchurch Congregational Chapel, *c.* 1903. The chapel, now the United Reformed Church, is the second building on the left just past the houses burnt down in the 1920s. There has been a strong tradition of nonconformity in Buntingford since the seventeenth century and there was once a Particular Baptist Chapel in Farringdon's Yard and a Quaker meeting house, location unknown.

*Above:* Wyddial Church and Vicarage, *c.* 1830. Much restored in the nineteenth century, the church of St. Giles has recently again needed considerable repair work. Inside are some interesting memorial brasses. The vicarage was demolished at some time in the nineteenth century and no traces remain.

*Left:* Throcking Church, *c.* 1830. Holy Trinity Church, Throcking, is very small. It has a most unusual tower built in the thirteenth century but completed in brick in 1660. The village of Throcking is today mostly modern buildings.

*Above:* Wyddial Church, *c.* 1912. The chancel chapel was built in 1532 of brick. There is a monument to Sir William Goulston who died in 1687. A priest is mentioned in the Domesday Book when the manor was held by Hardwin of Scales. In the twelfth century, the advowson was granted to the priory of Lewes.

*Right:* Throcking Church interior, *c.* 1830. Buntingford is partly in the parish of Throcking and the advowson of the Chapel of St. John the Baptist, Buntingford (replaced by St. Peter's), belonged to the lord of the manor of Throcking in the thirteenth century.

St. Peter's Chapel-of-Ease, *c.* 1790. Although now officially the parish church of Layston, St. Peter's was built as a chapel-of-ease to St. Bartholomew's, Layston, 1615–26, replacing the chapel of St. John the Baptist on the same site. The drawing by H.G. Oldfield shows St. Peter's in about 1790 and also offers a view of the bridge and part of the Almshouses. The pump, seen on page 22, is in the foreground.

St. Peter's, *c.* 1912. In this much later view, the alterations made in 1899–1900 which removed the two small turrets and added a porch and a bell tower can be seen. The parish clerk lived in the small cottage between the chapel and the bridge.

St. Peter's interior, c. 1912. The alterations had made the apse housing the altar higher. The altar, unusually, is at the south end of the chapel. Andrew Strange, the vicar from 1604, collected £418.13s.8d to build it and was left with 3s.7d when it was finished. It was licensed by the Bishop of London in 1626.

Clergy and choir at Layston, c. 1941. Rev Barff and his father, Canon Barff, with choir and church officials. Back row from left: John Bull, Bernard Smith, Mrs Pateman, George Hills, Charles Miles, Bonness, Jack Pateman, Mervyn Corp, Charlie Smith, Miss Marsden, Ralph Fisher, Gordon Miles. Sitting: Mrs Corp and Miss Langham.

St. Richard's R.C. Church, Saturday 16 May 1914. Mgr. R.H. Benson preaching at the laying of the foundation stone spoke of his great joy that his ideal of a local church was being realised. The sanctuary, nave and sacristy were the first to be built financed by Benson's many friends and well-wishers. Unfortunately, he never lived to enter the church as he died of pneumonia at Salford in October of that year and was buried in his garden at Hare Street.

St. Richard's R.C. Church, 1914. The church under construction built by Jacklin and Co. of Royston with George Handy of Buntingford as the local manager. He is seen in the foreground wearing a straw boater. The tower, porch, and presbytery were added later as funds were raised. The campaign suggested that one flint could be bought for one shilling.

St. Francis's Convent chapel altar 1921. The building at Hillside erected in 1878 to replace the old Grammar School had become a Home for Inebriates, and then in 1920 a convent school for mentally handicapped boys. The chapel shown here was replaced by a modern one and that too has now given way to a housing development.

Salvation Army band 1924. A citadel in Meeting Alley (now a pet food warehouse) was the base for an active S.A. presence in Buntingford during the first third of this century. The officers in this photo are Capt Doris Sweet and Lieut. Sara Moore. Other members include Mrs Harris, Florrie Bradford, Lily Plumb, Daniel Foster, Ben White, Mrs Hills, Mrs Parker, and Mrs Webb.

Grammar School, c. 1830. Buntingford Grammar School was founded sometime after 1620 by Elizabeth Freeman and Lady Jane Barkham, the daughters of John Crouch of Alswick Hall, at the instigation of Alexander Strange. Bishop Seth Ward was one of the more eminent pupils and in 1679 he gave £1,000 to found 4 scholarships. In 1878 when the school moved to Hillside, the building became a private house. The schoolmaster's house at right angles to the main building was added in the early eighteenth century.

Girls' School, c. 1905. Surnames of the girls have been given as, left to right: (back) Clark, Tottman, Smith, Jackson, Attwood, Geaves, Budd, Edwards, Webb; (centre) Marsden, Norris, Peacock, Hall, Moule, -?-; (front) Parker, Balls, Keen, Worboys, Mayes, Smith, Ward.

Boys' school, 1905. The third boy from the left in the front row is Jack Aylott and the boy on the left of the second row back is Tom Dellow. The schoolmaster is James Boniwell. The National (boys') school was built in 1845 for 140 pupils.

Boys' school: gardening, *c.* 1925. In the background is Mr. E.E. Dennis.

Infants' class, *c.* 1930. This classroom was demolished when Layston School was created from the old Buntingford J.M.I. School. Among the children in the front row are Ivy Gatwood, Ben Aylott, Ron Deards, Bill Reed, Walter Seymour; in the middle row, Eileen Harris and her brother, Sid Webb, Joan Beharrel, Len Neale, Joan Daniels, Lily Peacock; in the back row, Philip Plumb, Myrtle Mayes, David Haddock, John Handy, Frank Peacock.

Buntingford School, winners of the Musical Festival Banner 1930. E.E. Dennis, the headmaster, was an accomplished musical director and energetic organiser. Under his leadership, Buntingford won many musical awards. The accepted wisdom was that if he wore his grey suit at school he was in a good mood but beware the blue suit. Many years after his death, his widow said she had not been aware of this legend. Back from left: Joyce Woods, Herbie Parker, Doris King, Charlie Ross; middle: Stan Attwood, Irene Martin, Marion Mayes, Elsie Daniels, Lavinia Smith, Eric Martin; front: Forence Beharrel, Joan Sparkes, Doris Whitehouse, Flossie Darton.

# Three

# Houses and Other Buildings

Corneybury, c. 1910. The Manor of Corney was one of the principal estates in the area in Anglo-Saxon and Norman times. The Knights Templars owned land here and the great priory of Holy Trinity, London, received land and dues from Hugh Tricket in the twelfth century, having members of their foundation living and working here to manage their estates. Corneybury House is an early seventeenth-century brick house with parts rebuilt in 1681. It stands in a magnificent park which has been the setting for many Buntingford events over the years including the Agricultural and Horticultural Society shows which in some years attracted over ten thousand visitors. The River Rib flows through the Park, serenely for the most part but devastating when the floods came in 1968.

*Above*: The Red House, *c.* 1922. The Red House, now the headquarters of Churchills, Chartered Surveyors and Estate Agents, who have sponsored this book, was the home of Claud Fraser, London solicitor and Chairman of the old Buntingford Rural District Council. His eldest son, Claud Lovat Fraser, who died tragically young in 1921, was the renowned theatrical designer whose settings and costumes for the revival of *The Beggars Opera* at the Lyric Theatre, Hammersmith, changed the course of English stage design.

*Left*: Claud Lovat Fraser, 1920. Fraser painted and drew many scenes in the Buntingford area.

*Above:* Wall painting in the former Bell Inn. The Bell Inn ceased to be licensed about 1880 and is now dwelling houses and a shop. Some years ago, in the southern-most house, some Medieval wall-paintings were found over the fireplace in a living room. The paintings were judged to have been from two periods and the figure of the saint shown here is from the earlier group.

*Right:* Hannah Meredith's House. One of Claud Lovat Fraser's favourite subjects was Hannah Meredith's Cottage which stood on the site later occupied by the Women's Institute Hall (now a furniture showroom). Hannah kept many chickens which ran about everywhere including the High Street and into her kitchen where she made the chutney for which she was famed. She also had a pet lamb which followed her about everywhere even to the shops, Her father, James Meredith, who was a Schoolmaster, used to walk to Westmill twice each Sunday to keep the choir in order (with a stick it was recorded). During the sermon he used to read Bells Weekly News which he had tucked into his long coat before the service. Before one of his favourite hymns was played he would say in a loud voice "Now we're going to have a beauty". The late Bernard Miles could be imagined in the part.

Chapel and Almshouses, *c.* 1830. The drawing by J.C. Buckler is a good example of the artist's skill and portrays two of the finest seventeenth-century buildings in the county. Bishop Seth Ward's Hospital was built in 1684 as almshouses for four poor men and four poor women of the parishes of Layston and Aspenden. They have been used as such to this day and currently are being re-roofed, having the chimneys rebuilt, and having some carefully designed additions to the rear of the buildings.

Seth Ward. This portrait of Seth Ward, Bishop of Salisbury, was painted by John Greenhill, pupil of Lely, and for many years hung either in the central hall of the Almshouses or in St. Peter's Chapel. For its better conservation it is now deposited in the County Records Office, Hertford, where it can be seen on the wall of the public search room.

Ward's Hospital before 1910. Ward was the son of a Buntingford attorney, born in the town in the parish of Aspenden. After schooling in the Grammar School he went up to Cambridge as a precocious scholar. He became a renowned mathematician, astronomer and churchman. He was one of the founders of the Royal Society. After being Bishop of Exeter he was translated to Salisbury where he took the advice of his close friend, Christopher Wren, to save the famous spire of the cathedral from collapse.

Tercentenary celebrations. The almshouses may have been designed by Wren although there is no documentary proof. Some experts favour Robert Hooke (largely because of a cryptic entry in Hooke's diary). In 1984, the Trustees organised tercentenary celebrations. Speaking is Revd John Moore, Vicar of Layston and Aspenden. next to him is the Rt. Revd Kenneth Pillar, Bishop of Hertford. On the far left of the photo is Mrs Joan Bailey, Clerk and Treasurer to the Trustees.

Layston Vicarage, *c.* 1936. The present Vicarage Road is built on the site of the Layston Vicarage and gardens. The house was an impressive one from the outside and there was much room for meetings and other functions inside as well as attractive grounds for fêtes. Unfortunately, the interior left much to be desired and when Revd Alfred Howard resigned after about forty years, the living was turned down by twelve possible incumbents because of its state.

Aspenden Rectory, *c.* 1920. Although Layston and Aspenden parishes have been combined for some years. and in 1995 with Westmill, too,they were for centuries individual parishes. Aspenden Rectory has been a private house for 40 years or so. It probably dates from the late fifteenth century and is of exceptional interest as a purpose built rectory in the form of a late Medieval Wealden house with later additions.

Little Court, c. 1780. Now the only large house with extensive gardens left in the town, Little Court is of interest for being the house where Dr. John Addenbrooke lived with the Crouch family for the last few years of his short life, dying in 1719 at the age of 39, and leaving £4,500 to found the great hospital at Cambridge. In 1700, Henry Chauncey's History of Hertfordshire contained a large engraving of Little Court showing extensive formal gardens surrounding the then very large house. The River Rib flowing through the grounds was full of water and, apparently, fish.

Parish rooms and thatched house Royston Road, 1923. To the right of the picture is the parish room standing at the end of the vicarage drive. Here the county library had a few boxes of books to start the Buntingford library service in 1926. The room, of course, was also used for various parish meetings. On the left are Mrs Crouch and her daughter, then Reuben Woods, at his door.

The Bridewell and Old Croft, Wyddial Road, c. 1934. The house on the left is the former bridewell, or house of correction. Bridewells (named after the Bridewell in London) were set up in the sixteenth century to incarcerate beggars, vagrants and other undesirables and to hold people who might be facing serious charges at the assizes. The bridewell for the Hundreds of Edwinstree and Odsey was in Buntingford from the late sixteenth century until 1843. It was visited by John Howard, the prison reformer, on several occasions and he was critical of its sanitation and general condition.

River Rib, River Green Bridge and the Cage, c. 1907. The Cage is a small brick building which was used to imprison drunks and other miscreants for a short time, until sober perhaps. Built in the eighteenth century, this one was recently renovated by the Town Council and the Civic Society.

*Above:* Pig's Nose. The origins of the name of this stretch of the River Rib and of the thatched house alongside it are not entirely clear although traditionally supposed to be because of the shape of the rivercourse but this is not really so. The house was used as a poor house before the building of the Union Workhouse

*Right:* The Town Clock, *c.* 1908. Built over an archway and supported on the south by what was probably the Crowned Lyon Inn and on the north by the former Angel Inn, the town clock and the other two buildings were part of Henry Skynner's Bequest. The clock has only one hand.

43

Longmead, c. 1930. This large house with impressive gardens was formerly the residence of Herbert C. Marshall and his wife. Marshall had retired from the well-known London store of Marshall and Snelgrove and spent his time in local activities being in great demand to make presentations and preside over meetings and organisations. When the house was demolished its name was given to one of the smaller roads built over the site.

Family group, c. 1912 This impressive family photo is from the Harry A. Jackson "hoard" but despite much effort it has not yet been identified although several individual photos of those in the group also exist.

Layston Court staff, c. 1890.

Aspenden Hall, c. 1908. The original Aspenden Hall, illustrated in Chauncy's History, was the home of the Freeman family and Seth Ward spent part of the Civil War in semi-exile there. Later it became a school in which the historian, Thomas Macauley, boarded as a child. That building was replaced by the current house built in 1856 for Sir Henry Lushington. In 1963, the Hall was gutted for farm use but may once again become a dwelling.

Scotdale, London Road, c. 1920. Built for Miss Lushington, seen here, of the Aspenden Hall family. Renowned for her eccentric driving and clinging to ownership of ancient cars.

Layston Cottage, c. 1950. The snow sets off this early sixteenth-century house now divided into two dwellings at River Green. When the Buntingford and Hadham Rural Districts were abolished they were replaced by the Braughing R.D. although the Council met in Buntingford and Bishops Stortford. The B.R.D.C sat back while someone bought Layston Cottage and the huge garden for £3,000 and then paid the new owner £7,500 for one fifth of an acre to build the sheltered bungalow development "Ashfords".

The Causeway, c. 1909. Just around the corner from Layston Cottage were the thatched cottages on the Causeway leading to the schools and to Layston Church.

Aspenden Post Office, c. 1910. At this time the Post Office at Aspenden was run by Mrs Mary Poulton. It closed finally on 29 April, 1967. Miss Mould was the last postmistress. At one time there had been an evening delivery of mail at 7 p.m. The morning round had been changed from 8 a.m. to 9 a.m. as the first time was "too early" according to the residents.

Owles Hall, c. 1930. This handsome castellated house stands about one mile from Buntingford between Alswick Hall and Owles Farm. It was owned at the time of this photo by Dr. Shaw who was a skilled engineer specialising in model steam locomotives. It was rumoured that a previous owner in the First World War used to signal to German Zeppelins from the roof.

Layston House, c. 1960. Described in a sketch of 1839 as Watt's House, this later became the residence of Colonel Cuthbert and Lady Adela Larking, equerry and lady in waiting to the Duke and Duchess of Connaught who visited them in May, 1882, travelling on the Buntingford railway and being greeted by some 500 patriotic Buntingfordians. It was demolished not long after this photograph together with its imposing conservatories and stables. Snells Mead estate now occupies the site.

*Four*

# At Your Service!

Fire Brigade at Hoddesdon, August 25th 1905. The Buntingford Volunteer Fire Brigade was formed in 1896 after a public meeting held in the town opened a subscription list. £104.8s.4d. was raised from fifty subscribers including six insurance companies. A Merryweather fire engine was purchsed for £80 and there was no shortage of volunteers to man it. The Brigade won first prize at this district competition at Hoddesdon. The men are, from left to right: F. Hamilton (the first Captain), F. Brewington, F. Sharp, J. Cutts, P. Hamilton, A. Barham (Lieut.) and E.G. Thody who took over as Captain from Hamilton.

Volunteers, 1903. Normally drawn by a pair of horses, the brigade had to rely on man power if the horses couldn't be caught. Some thirty men were required to work the pumps when a convenient supply of water was available.

After a fire at the Mushroom Farm, Aspenden, *c.* 1903. The thirty pumpers were thirsty pumpers and had to be kept well supplied with refreshment. At one fire when they learnt that the police had drunk all the beer they walked out and left the police to do the pumping.

Fire Brigade at Hoddesdon, 1910. The fire engine was kept in a rather rickety shed behind the Angel Public House but it was always spruced up for the contests.

The new fire engine, 1931. Horses had become even more difficult to get and no one volunteered to risk their car in towing the engine. After a campaign waged largely by E.G. Thody in the local paper and at meetings, the Buntingford Rural District Council agreed to reform the Brigade and to purchase a modern motor fire engine. In front are E.G. Thody, Capt., J. Cutts , Bert Thody. Sitting on the engine from the left, Leslie Smith, Harry Handy, Jack Poulton, Jack Aylott. Standing at rear, Fred Handy. At rear, Joe Thody, Arthur Clark, F. Elliott, Stan Rayment.

The new Fire Station, 1931. A new engine required a new fire station and the B.R.D.C. built one in front of the Cosy Cinema (the Benson Hall). The formal opening was by Mr. H.C. Marshall (see p. 44). The poster behind is advertising the current cinema programme.

Fire Brigade, Jan 1942. Most of the 1931 Volunteers are still there but they have now been joined by younger men including their sons (for example John Handy third from the left).

Dr. Henry Edward Dixon, seen here in Wyddial about 1925, was said to be the last doctor in England to visit his patients on horseback. Whether this was so, or not, it is certain that he preferred to keep his Wednesday and Saturday surgeries brief so that he could get away to ride to the Puckeridge Hunt. His horse, Rayton, was an old steeplechaser. Dr. Dixon died in Royston Hospital in 1941 at the age of 93.

Isolation ambulance, 1936. When infectious diseases struck the locality, the Isolation Hospital on Rifford Hill between Aspenden and Westmill was opened up by the Buntingford R.D.C. and the patients conveyed in this horse-drawn ambulance which would have looked in place in Transylvania. George Aylott (driver), E.G.Thody next to him,Mrs. Bruce, the nurse, inside, and Jack Bruce, caretaker, on the right. The building is now known as Pinehill.

The Post Office, 1905. Since the first post was organised in 1603 on the London to Berwick-on-Tweed and Edinburgh Road, the Old North Road, Buntingford has owed much of its prosperity to its location on the road some thirty miles north of London. The staff and carts are lined up outside the old post office in the High Street opposite the Market hill.

Post Office, c. 1924. The Postmaster, Albion Callaway Bartlett (on right) and his deputy, George Smith, are shown in the doorway together with a telegraph boy. Bartlett retired in 1930 after 25 years in the post.

Post Office, Market Hill, c. 1928. Hagger and Cooper's coachmaking works and garage are on the right.

New post office in Baldock Road.

Railway Inn and Police, *c.* 1865 The building of the railway inspired the brewers E.K. and C. Fordham to open the Railway Inn a few yards from Buntingford Station in 1865. The police seemed to have taken an early interest in it. The photo is possibly of the opening of the pub judging from the early style of uniform

Police Station, 1903. The police station and sessions hall was built in 1881 with accommodation for a sergeant and two constables. At the time of the photograph Sergeant Joseph Hunt was in charge.

# Five

# Sporting Activities

Football team, c. 1905. Football has always been a major sport in Buntingford with the local club having periods of great success and others of less achievement. The football ground at the north end of the town was never owned by the club and has now been built over despite resistance by all the local authorities. On appeal, the government appointed inspector decided that what the town needed was not a green space within the boundaries where a highly popular sport could continue to be played but more houses. This team includes Arthur Wilson, with the ball, and behind him C.E. Harradence and, on his left, Bill Smith.

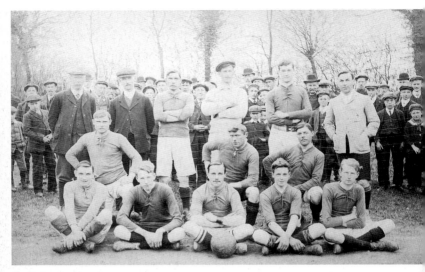

Football team, 1911.

Fancy dress football match, c. 1906. A valuable photo because it identifies the men in this fire brigade (skirts and bonnets) versus football club (top hats). Back row from left:
C.E. Harradence, H. Jackson. Next: G. Moss, E.M. Darville, W. Goldsmith, P. Wilson,
H. Wing, W. Smith, B. Lewis. Next: H. Aylott, F. Hamilton, W. Greaves, W. Warner,
A. Barham. E.G. Thody Next: F.W. Brooks, F.B. Sharp, C. Miles, J. Pateman, Front: L. Tyrrel,
H. Wilson, J. Cutts, E. Saunders, G. Attwood, W. Smith.

Football Club outside Union Workhouse, 1921. There are many photos of the Football Club extant but very few of the Union Workhouse, it was not a favourite subject for photographers. The setting of this picture was almost certainly because of the involvement with the club of the large man standing second from the right. This was F.W. Butler, Master of the Workhouse, who was also a special constable, captain of the Bowls Club, member of the British Legion, secretary/treasurer of the War Memorial Fund etc. From left, back row: W. Hatchett, M. Mapley, A. Dray, F. Camp (secretary), W. Smith, J. Rand, W. Budd. Middle row: W.Smith, G. Linsell, A. Clark, S. Smith, S. Bartlett, R. Rand, T. Moule, Neale, P. Reed, A.G. Day, F.W. Butler, J. Thody. Front row: A.C. Bartlett, Revd Jones, H. Handy, c. Smith, S. Thorogood, S. Howlett, H.C. Marshall (president), H. Clark, J. Moule, A. Wallace, R. May, E.J. Tottman, J. Pateman.

Aspenden Football Club, c. 1950. Included are Doug Jordan, Frank Knight, Doug Jackson, Peter Canfield, Chris Bradley, Bill Baker, and Alan Smith.

Buntingford Football Club, 1949. This is a mixture of the first and reserve teams In the back row are committee members from left: Herbie Howard, Mr. Buckle, Arthur Warner, Arthur Sullivan, John Parkes. Standing: Ben Aylott, Wally Smith, Ron Skeggs, Cyril Clayton, Les Poulton, Denis Saunders, Reg Clayton, Will Warner, Bernard Ansell, Stanley Ward. Sitting: Tom Rand, Len Neale, Frank Aylott, Doug Jordan, Jack Bishop (Chairman) Tom Morris, Sid Webb, Cuthbert Geaves, Peter Canfield. On grass, Chris McHugh and Frank Rand.

Buntingford Football Club, 1949. This picture of the Reserves was taken on the Football Ground (see page 57). From left standing: Arthur Guest, Denis Saunders, Wally Smith, Cuthbert Geaves, Ernie Leathers. Kneeling: Frank Rand, Philip Plumb, Tom Morris. Sitting: Will Warner, Len Neale, George Warner, Terry Heath, Tim Smith.

Buntingford Blue Bells, c. 1960. Ladies' football team with some male help. Part of the Carnival Week.

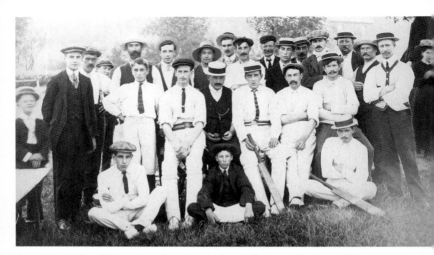

Aspenden Cricket Club, c. 1910. The cricket section of the Aspenden Sports Club was formed in April, 1909, and cricket has been played on the Green nearly every season since. In the centre, with the bat, is Arthur Wilson, married into the Poulton family and later to be proprietor of the garage in Buntingford now Smith's.

Aspenden Cricket Club, c. 1960. Tim Rayment is the umpire, team members include John Crane, Reg and Cyril Clayton, Les Mole, Bob Skipp, Jimmy Rand, and Alan Warner.

Tennis Club, *c.* 1912

Tennis Club, *c.* 1923. In the back row are Bert Thody, Arthur Wilson, Wilf Smith. In the next row on the left are Leslie Smith and Stan Smith. Also included are Mary Wilson, Elsie Geaves, Esmé Aylott, and Ivy Howlett.

The Buntingford Bowls Club was formed in 1923 and at first played on the lawn at Layston Cottage. The present ground was opened in 1926. Bowls was, however, played earlier. The Club in the 1960s included, back: Bob Hudgell, Reg Powell, Ted Devonshire, C. Tomkins, F. Bardwell, John Skinner, M. Rolf, H. Parker, B. Ansell; front: Dennis Webb, Ron Brown, Tom West, Tom Gray, Mervyn Corp, Wilf Downham, Bob Smith.

Shooting party, c. 1900. The location is not certain but various familiar Buntingford figures are in the photo.

Angling at Scots Green, Aspenden, *c.* 1900. E.E. Darville, the Buntingford newsagent and stationer and publisher of picture postcards, is fishing in the Rib while his wife looks on from the footbridge. Trout found their way upstream to Aspenden from Coles Park.

Coach trip, *c.* 1923. With few people owning cars, coach trips were popular and this was on the way to Coombe Martin. The Buntingford Belle was advertised as taking trippers to the British Empire Exhibition at Wembley in 1924.

Puckeridge Hounds, Market Hill, Saturday 25 March 1911. Buntingford is very much in Puckeridge Hunt country and the hounds met frequently in the town and at Layston Church.

Sunday Outing, c. 1912. This group of young men in their best suits consists of (back left to right) Harry Rayment, Ralph Fisher, Fred Patmore, Walter (Jim) Plumb. Front: Ernie McNulty, Harry Wakefield, Fred Seymour. Five joined up a year or two later: all returned although Jim Plumb was severely wounded by shrapnel and spent many years in hospital afterwards.

## Six

# Recreation and Leisure

Buntingford Dramatic Society in *The Blue Goose*, March 1951. The Dramatic Society was reformed after the Second World War and produced many plays in a few years. Although there were some serious pieces like *Outward Bound*, most were comedies and farces which suited the talents of the company. On one occasion the author of the play not only braved a performance but was happy to announce from the stage at the end that he thought it had been better performed than the original West End production. Peter Blackmore, author of *Miranda*, the mermaid play, who lived at Sandon, is seen in the centre of the cast and backstage staff of one of his other plays, *The Blue Goose*, which he also enjoyed. In the front they are from the left Millie Rand, Irene Harris, Phyllis Noble, Sylvia Rasbary, Betty Buckingham, Blackmore, Zoe Ryder, Sally Roff, Eunice Clark, Margaret Phillips, Joan Brickley, Mavis Hearne. At the back, George Bailey, Ernie Williams, Eric Brownless, Cyril Berry, Bob Stringer, Ernest Howard, Philip Plumb (producer).

The Town Band, 1897. The Town Silver Band originated in the old Drum and Fife band. Mr. Worrall, an assistant at the chemist's shop, started it to find something for young men to do, other than cricket. Worral is in top hat and evening dress, the others are in Hussars' uniform and standing from L. to R. are Suttersley, Sale, Drage, Neale, May, Cutts, Smith, Saunders, Marsden, Miles, Harradence, Mayhew, and Cutts. Sitting: Pateman, H.Saunders, Cutts, T. Saunders, W. Miles and Hamilton.

Band outside Foresters' Hall, c. 1907. There were various friendly societies in the town in the nineteenth and early twentieth centuries. There was a branch of the Ancient Order of Foresters here and it had its own premises, the Foresters' Hall, in Baldock Road (where a hairdressing salon now stands). Here the Foresters' Court was held and the hall was available for other functions.

Band at the Show, 1921. The Town Brass Band, as it was originally, became the Silver Band, and was expected to be at all appropriate functions. In 1921 the long established Horticultural Society and the newly established Agricultural Society had a combined show in Corneybury Park. One of the large marquees housing the flower show is seen in the background.

Fête, c. 1923. Music making was not only of the brass band type and here is a smaller combination playing at one of the many fêtes held each summer in the town when there were so many large gardens as the venue.

Buntingford Town Silver Band, c. 1930. The original Brass Band obtained its instruments from a firm in Newbury on the instalment system. In 1925 they set about raising money to become the Silver Band and many functions were held to raise the money to buy the new instruments.

Orchestra at Westmill, c. 1933. For this fête at Westmill the theme was the eighteenth century and the orchestra obliged. In front from the left: Mrs Bright, Marjorie Wallace, Violet Miller, Myrtle Wornham, Harry Mayes. Back row: Mr Bright, Mr Smith, Albert King, Jack Parker, Fred Anthony, Jim Plumb, Ted Saunders, Tommy Wornham and Keith Bright.

*Above: Robinson Crusoe*, January 1932 The Buntingford Bow Bells' pantomine, in the Benson Hall. The musical director was E.E. Dennis and dances arranged by Joan Newbury. Back row from left: Doris Bush, Jack Poulton, Joy Howlett, Esme Smith, Mr Scrivener,Leslie Smith, -?-; middle row: Sylvia Poulton, Sydney Daniels, Nellie Scott, Sid Howlett, Miss Henry, Mrs Bert Thody, Myrtle Wornham, Mary Fell, Molly Wornham, Bert Thody, Herbert Cutts, Mrs Daniels, Joe Thody, L.Walsingham, Millie Rand. Front row: May Scrivener, Flossie Darton, Elsie Daniels, V .Hamilton, Sheila Armstrong, Doris Harvey, Joyce Woods, Norah Piggott, Sylvia Ward.

*Right:* Herbert Cutts, the postman, in pantomime (*Ali Baba?*)

Didelem and Katchem 1921. One of the many fêtes held that summer had this white elephant stall run by F.W. Butler, the Workhouse Master (far left) and Revd J. Reynolds Jones, Congregational Minister, helped by young Colin Handy and Emrys Jones with Leslie Smith as customer.

Buntingford and District Agricultural Society.

President 1922 · Sir Charles Nall-Cain, Bart., J.P.

# 3rd ANNUAL SHOW

At CORNEY BURY PARK, BUNTINGFORD

(By kind permission of W. J. Wedd, Esq.) on

THURSDAY, JULY 20th, 1922,

In conjunction with Buntingford & District Horticultural Society's
Flower Show.

## Official Catalogue.

Hon. Secretary : G. SCARBOROUGH TAYLOR, High Street, Buntingford.
Telephone : HUNTINGFORD 20.

### PRICE ONE SHILLING & SIXPENCE.

Third Annual Show, 1922. Buntingford and District Agricultural Society was formed in June 1920 and immediately planned to run a show in conjunction with the Horticultural Society which was much older, holding shows since 1884. The show was a great success, In the one day, a Thursday, 6,500 went through the gates. For a few years this co-operation continued but later the agricultural show split off and went its own way.

Carnival dance, W.I. Hall, 1960. The Women's Institute Hall was a popular venue for many functions including this dance held at the end of Carnival Week. The Hall is now converted to a furniture show-rooms at the north end of the town. Stan Attwood, the Carnival organiser. who ran a dance band, is seen in the background to the left of the man with the mike.

Carnival, 1960. Bob Skipp, vice-chairman of the Carnival Committee, visiting celebrity Peter Bryant, of the BBC Groves Family, Jessie Attwood, wife of the carnival organiser and their daughter, Beverly, on the Football Field with the Women's Institute Hall in the left background.

Carnival, 1970. The carnival procession went from Hillside through the High Street to the Football Field, or later, to the Playing Fields. The Carnival Queen, Patricia Edens, presided over the week's festivities, with her princesses (Anne Cornes on the right).

Carnival 1970. The Cubs' float: Oliver Twist. Much work by parents and helpers was needed to make the costumes and furnish the float.

Variety Show, 1967. Buntingford Dramatic Society perform a variety of turns at the W.I. Hall. Eric Brownless leads the company in songs from H.M.S. *Pinafore*. From left, Anna Miles, Charlie Edwards, Mavis Pegram, Olive Green, Elizabeth West.

Benson Hall, c. 1924. Built as the parish hall for St. Richard's Catholic Church, the hall needed to make money for the parish and was widely used for dances, whist-drives, shows and particularly films. It became the Cosy Cinema in 1936 and enjoyed great popularity during the Second World War. It also provided the venue for concerts and pantomines which, despite the small stage, were always much enjoyed.

Buntingford Women's Institute January 1920. The town W.I. started in November 1918 but the first annual meeting was held in January, 1920. The photo was taken in the yard of the George Hotel following the meeting in the Assembly Room above. A membership of 116 had been attained.

W.I. Group Meeting at Aspenden House, 5 August 1926. Some 200 members of the Buntingford Group of the W.I. met at Aspenden House, the home of Capt. and Mrs. H.H. Williams, hoping to enjoy the beautiful gardens. Heavy showers drove them indoors where even that large number were accommodated for tea and entertainment. The weather cleared during the evening so that this photograph could be taken on the lawn.

*Seven*

# Trade and Industry

Railway station and sawmill, 1929. Buntingford's prosperity through the centuries has depended on the trade engendered through its position on the Old North Road. As circumstances changed, including the greater use of the other road to the north through Baldock etc., prosperity declined and the coming of the railways was another challenge to be met. Local landowners and tradesmen raised money to build the Ware, Hadham and Buntingford Railway. The sawmill, middle left, was in the field used for the annual fairs in the 1930s.

Bridge, before 1936. The hump-backed bridge drew much criticism because drivers tended to speed over it causing much danger to other road users. The key stones bore the initials NM and WE, date 1766, and these are Nehemiah Mayes of Buntingford and William Edwards of Braughing, both bricklayers, and recorded as doing work on various bridges in the district. The cottage on the left was the Turnpike House where the tolls for using the turnpike road were collected. This building was demolished well before the new bridge was started.

New bridge, 1937. The new bridge, which necessitated the demolition of two cottages standing where the bus shelter is now, was opened in 1937. It incorporated the two keystones mentioned above. On the right is the Jolly Sailors public house.

The wealthier residents owned cars such as this, seen at Owles Hall, together with a chauffeur to drive them.

Railway station, c. 1870. The station master in full uniform, can be seen together with top-hatted men, probably some of those responsible for getting the railway built. The first train left on 3 July 1863 and it is possible that this photo was taken not long after the opening.

Buntingford station, c. 1912. Little had changed since the earlier picture except for the addition of posters advertising various services and excursions.

Buntingford station platform and rolling stock, c. 1903. The railway stopped at Buntingford although there were various proposals for extending it to Royston and Cambridge which came to nothing.

*Right:* Changeover from steam to diesel 1959. Bernard Ansell, the driver, and his fireman, in the last steam loco to pull the passenger trains, talk to Albert Vandome, a local district and parish councillor. Tom Gray in the driving seat of the new three-car diesel powered Rolls Royce units which took over.

*Below:* Time-table, Buntingford Branch line 1960. Although the line was not profitable in modern times, it did not make the losses claimed under the Beeching proposals. The figures used to justify its closure were "massaged", to use a euphemism, in a way in which no businessman would have dared if he wished to keep out of prison.

### ST. MARGARET'S and BUNTINGFORD [1960]
#### (Diesel Trains—Second class only)

**MONDAYS TO FRIDAYS**

| | a.m. | a.m. | a.m. | a.m. | p.m. | p.m. | p.m. | p.m. | | p.m. | |
|---|---|---|---|---|---|---|---|---|---|---|---|
| LIVERPOOL STREET .... dep | 4 52 | 5 32 | 6 52 | 8 12 | 2 42 | 4 12 | 5 12 | 6 12 | .. | 8 42 | ... |
| Broxbourne and H. .. " | 5 28 | 6 8 | 7 28 | 8 48 | 3 18 | 4 48 | 5 50 | 6 50 | .. | 9 18 | ... |
| ST. MARGARET'S .... dep | 5 44 | 6 53 | 7 53 | 8 58 | 3 33 | 5 26 | 2 7 | 3 | .. | 9 33 | ... |
| Mardock .......... " | 5 48 | .. | .. | 9 2 | 3 37 | 5 6 | 6 7 | 7 | .. | 9 37 | ... |
| Widford .......... " | 5 51 | .. | .. | 9 5 | 3 40 | 5 9 | 6 9 | 7 10 | .. | 9 40 | ... |
| Hadham .. .. .. " | 5 55 | 7 0 | 8 0 | 9 8 | 3 43 | 5 12 | 6 12 | 7 13 | .. | 9 43 | ... |
| Standon .......... " | 6 0 | 7 6 | 8 6 | 9 14 | 3 49 | 5 18 | 6 18 | 7 19 | .. | 9 49 | ... |
| Braughing .......... " | 6 3 | 7 8 | 8 8 | 9 16 | 3 51 | 5 20 | 6 20 | 7 21 | .. | 9 51 | ... |
| West Mill .......... " | 6 6 | .. | .. | 9 20 | 3 55 | 5 24 | 6 24 | 7 25 | .. | .. | ... |
| BUNTINGFORD .... arr | 6 9 | 7 14 | 8 14 | 9 23 | 3 58 | 5 27 | 6 27 | 7 28 | .. | 9 57 | ... |

**SATURDAYS ONLY**

| | a.m. | a.m. | a.m. | a.m. | a.m. | a.m. | p.m. | p.m. | p.m. | p.m. | p.m. | p.m. | p.m. |
|---|---|---|---|---|---|---|---|---|---|---|---|---|---|
| LIVERPOOL STREET .... dep | 4 52 | 5 32 | 6 52 | 8 12 | 10 52 | 12 22 | 1 32 | 2 52 | 4 12 | 5 12 | 6 12 | 8 52 | ... |
| Broxbourne and H. .. " | 5 28 | 6 8 | 7 28 | 8 48 | 11 28 | 1 8 | 2 8 | 3 28 | 4 50 | 5 50 | 6 48 | 9 28 | ... |
| ST. MARGARET'S .... dep | 5 44 | 6 53 | 7 53 | 8 58 | 11 38 | 1 20 | 2 20 | 3 38 | 5 26 | 2 7 | 3 9 | 38 | ... |
| Mardock .......... " | 5 48 | .. | .. | 9 2 | 11 42 | 1 24 | 2 24 | 3 42 | 5 6 | 6 7 | 7 9 | 42 | ... |
| Widford .......... " | 5 51 | .. | .. | 9 5 | 11 45 | 1 27 | 2 27 | 3 45 | 5 9 | 6 9 | 7 10 | 9 45 | ... |
| Hadham .. .. .. " | 5 55 | 7 0 | 8 0 | 9 8 | 11 48 | 1 30 | 2 30 | 3 48 | 5 12 | 6 12 | 7 13 | 9 48 | ... |
| Standon .......... " | 6 0 | 7 6 | 8 6 | 9 14 | 11 54 | 1 36 | 2 36 | 3 54 | 5 18 | 6 18 | 7 19 | 9 54 | ... |
| Braughing .......... " | 6 3 | 7 8 | 8 9 | 11 56 | 1 38 | 2 38 | 3 56 | 5 20 | 6 20 | 7 21 | 9 56 | ... | ... |
| West Mill .......... " | 6 6 | .. | .. | 9 20 | 12 0 | 1 42 | 2 42 | 4 0 | 5 24 | 6 24 | 7 25 | ... | ... |
| BUNTINGFORD .... arr | 6 9 | 7 14 | 8 14 | 9 23 | 12 3 | 1 45 | 2 45 | 4 3 | 5 27 | 6 27 | 7 28 | 10 2 | ... |

**MONDAYS TO FRIDAYS**

| | a.m. | a.m. | a.m. | a.m. | p.m. | p.m. | p.m. | p.m. | | p.m. | |
|---|---|---|---|---|---|---|---|---|---|---|---|
| BUNTINGFORD........ dep | 6 22 | 7 22 | 8 22 | 9 28 | 2 05 | 3 46 | 3 47 | 5 8 | .. | 10 2 | ... |
| West Mill .......... " | 6 24 | 7 24 | 8 24 | 9 30 | 4 22 | .. | 8 | 0 | .. | .. | ... |
| Braughing .......... " | 6 28 | 7 28 | 8 28 | 9 34 | 4 26 | 5 39 | 6 39 | 4 | .. | 10 7 | ... |
| Standon............ " | 6 30 | 7 30 | 8 30 | 9 36 | 4 28 | 5 42 | 6 42 | 8 | 6 | .. | 1010 |
| Hadham .......... " | 6 36 | 7 36 | 8 36 | 9 42 | 4 34 | 5 47 | 6 47 | 8 | 12 | .. | 1015 |
| Widford .......... " | 6 39 | 7 39 | 8 39 | 9 45 | 4 37 | .. | .. | 8 | 15 | .. | ... |
| Mardock .......... " | 6 42 | 7 42 | 8 42 | 9 48 | 4 40 | .. | .. | 8 | 18 | .. | ... |
| ST. MARGARET'S .... arr | 6 47 | 7 47 | 8 47 | 10 | 4 45 | 5 53 | 6 53 | 8 | 23 | .. | 1021 |
| Broxbourne and H. .. arr | 6 58 | 7 58 | 8 58 | 10 8 | 4 58 | 6 18 | 7 | 8 38 | .. | 1039 | ... |
| LIVERPOOL STREET .. " | 7 36 | 8 36 | 9 36 | 1046 | 5 36 | 6 56 | 7 46 | 9 16 | .. | 1116 | ... |

**SATURDAYS ONLY**

| | a.m. | a.m. | a.m. | a.m. | p.m. | p.m. | p.m. | p.m. | p.m. | p.m. | p.m. | p.m. |
|---|---|---|---|---|---|---|---|---|---|---|---|---|
| BUNTINGFORD........ dep | 6 22 | 7 22 | 8 22 | 9 42 | 12 22 | 1 50 | 3 | 2 4 | 20 | 5 34 | 6 34 | 7 58 |
| West Mill .......... " | 6 24 | 7 24 | 8 24 | 9 44 | 22 | 3 | 4 22 | 8 | 0 | ... | ... | ... |
| Braughing .......... " | 6 28 | 7 28 | 8 28 | 9 48 | 12 28 | 1 55 | 3 | 4 26 | 5 39 | 6 39 | 8 4 | 1012 |
| Standon............ " | 6 30 | 7 30 | 8 30 | 9 50 | 12 30 | 1 58 | 3 10 | 4 28 | 5 42 | 6 42 | 8 6 | 1015 |
| Hadham .......... " | 6 36 | 7 36 | 8 36 | 9 56 | 12 36 | 2 3 | 3 16 | 4 34 | 5 47 | 6 47 | 8 12 | 1020 |
| Widford .......... " | 6 39 | 7 39 | 8 39 | 9 59 | 12 39 | .. | 3 19 | 4 37 | .. | .. | 8 15 | ... |
| Mardock .......... " | 6 42 | 7 42 | 8 42 | 10 2 | 12 42 | .. | 3 22 | 4 40 | .. | .. | 8 18 | ... |
| ST. MARGARET'S .... arr | 6 47 | 7 47 | 8 47 | 10 7 | 12 47 | 2 9 | 3 27 | 4 45 | 5 53 | 6 53 | 8 23 | 1026 |
| Broxbourne and H. .. arr | 6 58 | 7 58 | 8 58 | 1018 | 1258 | 2 18 | 3 38 | 4 58 | 6 18 | 7 18 | 8 39 | 1038 |
| LIVERPOOL STREET .. " | 7 36 | 8 36 | 9 36 | 1056 | 1 36 | 2 56 | 4 16 | 5 36 | 6 56 | 7 56 | 9 16 | 1116 |

Connecting services are shown in light type.
**NO SUNDAY SERVICE**

Scouts on station, Sept 1939. The Buntingford troop of Boy Scouts on Buntingford Station on their way to Hunstanton for their summer camp. On the left of the group are Skipper W.B. Barber, a railwayman, his wife who was the Cub's Akela and their son. At the back from the left are David Haddock, Peter Thody, Bernard Ansell, John Handy, George Saunders. In front: Ben Aylott and Reg Mayes.

London County and Westminster Bank, 1914. One of two banks in the town at that time this branch was open for two hours on Friday mornings. The Gateway store now occupies the site. The cash is being delivered in a wheelbarrow (Photograph published by permission of NatWest Group Archives).

Steamwagon crashes, 13 Feb 1930. Why did the steam lorry laden with 15 tons of Eastwood's cement crash into the newly opened Electricity Showrooms in the High Street? The second photo shows why. Mr. Harry Handy was driving a Morris truck up Church Street (then two-way) into the High Street as the Foden was travelling south along the main road. They met and the Morris went into Pearce's bakers shop and the other lorry into the Showrooms. No one was seriously hurt.

C.H.Poulton's milk cart, c. 1925. A young Jack Poulton in front. My paternal grandmother, Mrs Watson, who then lived in Baldock Road, used to give the horse biscuits when the milkman called. If she was not waiting at the door, the horse would rattle the door knob with its teeth.

Harry A.Jackson, c. 1912. Harry A Jackson was a butcher in the High Street (there was another butcher Jackson in Church Street),who was an enthusiastic and skilled photographer and published some postcards (see page 113).

W.H. Smith, *c.* 1912. W.H. Smith was a general furnisher and dealer who had a shop in the High Street, next to the Black Bull. In the cart are his sons Wilfred and Leslie.

W.H. Smith's shop, 1895. The shop specialised in china and it is reliably reported that one day a bull broke loose and rampaged through the shop.

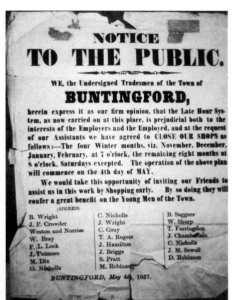

*Left*: Notice to the public, 1857. Of the signatories, B. Wright was a grocer, earthenware dealer and tallow chandler; Crowder, grocer; West and Norris, grocers and linendrapers; Bray, chemist; Lock, draper; Patmore, grocer and draper; Dix, linendraper; G. Nicholls, tailor and draper; c. Nicholls, postmaster and bookseller; J.Wright, saddler and harnessmaker; Gray, bricklayer and shopkeeper; Rogers, tailor and draper; Hamilton, ironmonger; Briggs (possibly Biggs) brewer cooper; Pratt, shopkeeper; Robinson, beer retailer; Saggers, joiner and builder; Sharp, beer retailer; Farringdon (or ton), boot and shoe maker; Chamberlain, victualler (Fox and Duck); c. Nicholls, cooper and brewer; Sewell, clock and watchmaker and jeweller; Robinson, beer retailer.

*Below*: Billhead of Spinks, 1860's. Successor of Crowder.

The Fox, Aspenden, *c.* 1893. Walter William Bunce, landlord of the Fox from 1886 to his death in December 1912, with his step-son, Walter Arnold aged 14. As well as being a beer retailer, Bunce was also a general shop-keeper.

Matthews Shop, *c.* 1900. Walter Matthews was a draper and outfitter in the shop where there is now the library. Next to it is the Globe public house. On the right is West View, whose extensive gardens at the back, particularly the lawn, were used for many local functions including summer dances.

Fitch's Eating House, c. 1900. Despite the name this was not a restaurant but a sweet shop, later the same under Joseph May and then his son-in-law Cecil Tottman when it was known as Totties'. Now a ladies hairdresser.

J. Smith and Son, Grocer, c. 1924. A current advert in the local paper offered three outstanding lines: Sardines, per large tin, 6d; Loose Cocoa, best quality, per lb 1/- and Dunmow Flitch Pure Lard, 1/- per lb.

Feasey's grocery shop, *c.* 1910. In the early years of this century, Frederick Feasey, a keen supporter of the Congregational Chapel, owned four grocery shops in Buntingford. One at the lower end of Church Street, and three in the High Street. He and his two sons used to attend Sunday service in their silk hats, frock coats and boots. Feasey went round the big houses of the neighbourhood by pony and trap to solicit orders on Mondays and later in the week the deliveries would be made by horse and van. The shops were open from 7.30 a.m. to 7.30 p.m.

Opening of the Co-operative Stores 1936. The reigning Co-op Queen accompanied Mr L. Monk, J.P., who performed the ceremony.

Aspenden Water Mill, *c.* 1900. The watermill has been non-working for many years but records of a mill here go back to at least the seventeenth century and it remained in the ownership of the same family, Boddy and Knight, until recent housing developments . It has recently been restored and additions made at the rear. Remnants of the mechanism are still housed in the section on the right.

Tumbling bays, *c.* 1923. Part of the arrangement for diverting the River Rib to the mill stream (now filled in) to turn the water wheel. The pool in front known as Sandy Hole has served as a natural swimming pool and was very popular during the Second World War with servicemen stationed locally.

Tannery, 1929. One of the biggest employers in Buntingford until its closure in 1925, the tannery was owned from 1854 by George Mickley who made good profits from it and was one of the main proponents of the Buntingford Railway. Henry Ashford bought the business in 1894 and on his retirement to Layston Cottage in 1918 it was acquired by a company which went bankrupt in 1925.

Demolition of maltings, c. 1910. Although not a major industry in the town, there were at least three maltings here in the nineteenth century. This one behind the Gate House in the High Street is being demolished under the supervision of E.G. Thody, the Surveyor to the Buntingford Rural District Council.

Harvesting, *c.* 1928. Cutting corn with a tractor and binder, the forerunner of the combine harvester, just outside Buntingford.

Haymaking, *c.* 1912. Not the usual dress for farm labourers but obviously some special occasion for Harry Jackson's family and friends.

Ploughing, *c.* 1920. The ploughman with three Suffolk Punch horses and a single furrow plough may be Harry Pegram who was always pleased to have his horses photographed when the opportunity arrived.

Harvesting, 1966. Ben Aylott, second son of an old Buntingford family, farmed at Buntingford and Hare Street before being ordained in the Church of England. His last harvest was at Hillside, just south of St. Francis's Convent.

Workmen, 1901. A pause for the camera in digging trenches for the new piped water supply provided by the Buntingford Rural District Council in 1907.

Workmen, c. 1890. On the left is George Attwood.

Building workers, *c.* 1910. Cyril Robinson is fifth from the right.

Painters and decorators at Hamels, *c.* 1910. The group includes J. Pateman, L. Sanders, E. Baker, G. Smith, W. Squires, F. Camp, G. Linsell, J. Francis, A. Marsden, and Mr. Footman.

F. Feasey's shop and cart, c. 1900. This was another of Feasey's shops, next to the London County and Westminster Bank (see page 82). The van driver was the grandfather of George Conyard and the boy was to become the father of Eddie Winters. In the doorway, Sam Saggers.

Haycarts passing the Adam and Eve, 1923. At the beginning of the century, horse-drawn loads of hay would be driven up to the stables in London. Local carters, like the late Fred Ward, made the journey twice a week, the journey each way taking a day and a half, sleeping in the wagon and returning home with a load of manure from the stables These carts were probably making local journeys.

*Eight*

# Places of Refreshment

The Angel Inn and the White House, *c.* 1903. Although today the large house on the left is the White House, this is a comparatively recent naming. Originally the White House was the newsagents and stationers shop, the other building supporting the Town Clock. Where there is now the town car park was at one time the Angel Orchard. Quoit playing took place in the Angel Yard behind the inn and, of course, the manual fire-engine was housed there.

*Above:* George and Dragon Hotel, *c.* 1903. The longest-lived of the town's two main hostelries (the Bell closed about 1880) it flourished until after the Second World War. Either may have been the inn where Pepys's wife became very ill. The George was the meeting place of the Trustees of the Wadesmill Turnpike, the first turnpike road.

*left:* George and Dragon, *c.* 1924. The inn-sign was of wrought iron and very heavy and ornate. In the nineteenth century, the establishment included a row of cottages in Church Street which housed hotel staff. In Victorian times, every train was met by horse-drawn broughams. The George was a great favourite with commercial travellers. The gateway has survived the alterations to the use of the buildings.

Former Bell Inn, c. 1923. In its heyday, the Bell was a most important posting inn with stables covering the present site of the Technical Institute and, across the other side of Baldock Road, Bell Barns, now a small industrial site. In 1669, Mary Edwards, Innkeeper of the Bell, issued her own halfpenny pieces as did other traders in the town and elsewhere to meet the shortage of official small change.

The Swan, 22 June 1911. All the public houses and shops were decorated for the coronation of King George V. The Swan probably dates from before the creation of Norfolk Road sometime in the middle of the nineteenth century as it has no windows on the Norfolk Road side.

The Fox and Duck, c 1912 The Fox and Duck was an alehouse in 1711 and got its present name in 1743. James Chamberlain was the licensee from 1846 to 1887 when his daughter, Mrs Fanny Brewington took over until 1936. She and her husband, who was a saddler for the Puckeridge Hunt, always kept a couple of young hounds at their house.

The Chequers, 1906. This has been a licensed house since at least 1750, when Susan Ingrey, widow, was in charge.

The White Hart, *c.* 1934. Was named in a will of 1600 when money was left to "poor people living in the White Hart yard". It was a base for the carters making their lengthy journeys to London at the beginning of the century. The bicycling gentleman with the white beard was a familiar sight around the town. He was the son of Revd John Henry Butt, vicar of Layston for fifty years, and was born in the Vicarage in 1858. He returned to live in Buntingford from Cheltenham in 1932 and died here in 1939.

The Angel, *c.* 1920. A view from the other direction. James Henry Jackson was licensee of the Angel for about 35 years. He died in about 1925 and his widow went to live at Owles Farm with her only surviving daughter, Mrs. R. Scott. The last licensee was Bob Hodson.

The Crown 22 June 1911. More decorations for the coronation of King George V. The present building is from the mid-nineteenth century but the establishment has been supposedly identified as the Crowned Lion held by Deodatus Bunyan in 1631.

Crown, c. 1924. Gas was supplied to the street lamps and the town generally from a gasworks near the railway station.

# Nine

# Occasions and People

The Relief of Mafeking in 1900 during the Second Boer War was greeted with great rejoicing locally, not only with normal patriotic feelings but because many local men were serving in South Africa. These included L. Fox, Tom Fox, E. Hatchett, T. Plumb, C. Conyard, Tom Conyard, F. Copcoat, and C. Edwards, the last named being in the Balloon Section of the Royal Engineers. Concerts were held to raise funds to provide comforts for the troops and the Vicar of Layston, Revd Alfred Howard, gave a series of lantern lectures at the Girls' School "to help the war effort". The photo shows the flags out when the news of the Relief came through. "The Indian Star" public house can also be seen on the left of the picture.

Celebrations on Market Hill, 6 July 1893. Taken by E.G. Thody from the scaffolding used to build the new Barclays Bank on the Market Hill. The occasion was the Duke of York's Wedding Day. St Peter's is seen before reconstruction and over the bridge where now stands Smith's Garage are maltings, long since demolished.

Procession 16 May 1914. Prior to the laying of the Foundation Stone of St. Richard's Church this procession of clergy marched down the High Street past the Market Hill and Layston Dairy to the site in Adam and Eve Field.

Market Hill 20 May 1910. Buntingford Band playing the 'Dead March' in Saul on the death of King Edward VII.

Proclamation of the new king 2 June 1910. In the words of the newspaper report "The proclamation of His Majesty King George V took place in the ancient and loyal town of Buntingford at 1 p.m. in the presence of an unusually large crowd of townspeople." Mr. F.C. Porter, J.P., Chairman of the Buntingford District Council was preceded by the Buntingford Boy Scouts. The Fire Brigade were on parade but unfortunately three parts of the members of the Town Band were working away preventing the Band from taking part, to universal disappointment. A gentleman of the town had thoughtfully provided a supply of buns with which to regale the schoolchildren.

Presentation, c. 1904. This is a presentation but what and where is not known although it appears to be H.C. Marshall making the presentation.

Bert Thody, c. 1930. Bert Thody, one of the three sons of E.G. Thody who figures so prominently throughout this book, was the guardian of Buntingford's past. He collected photographs, stories and artefacts and wrote entertainingly in parish magazines and local newspapers including the Buntingford and North East Herts Gazette. He was also a stalwart of the British Legion and the Buntingford Union Association and of many other local activities.

Group, c. 1925. In this group are E.E. Dennis, H. Clarke (Manager Labour Exchange) and Ernie Crane (coal-merchant) but the reason for the group is not clear.

Sir Harold Williams, c. 1960. Lived at Aspenden House from the early 1920s and played a prominent part in county, district and local matters. He was Chairman of the Hertfordshire County Council. Internationally, he was a renowned scholar of Dean Swift's writings.

May Day 1911. Mayers' Song. Twenty-five or more verses were song by those people who celebrated the First of May in the streets of the villages and towns of Hertfordshire in the early years of the nineteenth century. Most of the verses were common to the different parts of the county but there were some additional verses sung. The Buntingford extra verse was "There's a tuft lies at your head dear man, And another at your feet, Your good words and your good deeds Will altogether meet." Ruby Tottman sent this card to her brother after they had paraded through the streets and had their photo taken on West View Lawn.

Tariff Reform fête, 1911. Political activity before the First World War was concentrated heavily on Liberal Free Trade versus Conservative Tariff Reform. Buntingford was a strong centre for the latter and many fund raising functions were held including this fete and rally in Corneybury Park.

Election, 1929. Guy Kindersley, the Conservative candidate in the General Election of May 1929 shown with supporters and party workers outside the Tudor House in the High Street. Capt. H.H. Williams, later Sir Harold, is to our left of the doorway in which appears Bert Thody (left). On the extreme left of the photo is Revd Alfred Howard, Vicar of Layston. Kindersley (in the bow tie) was elected but Labour formed the Government even though polling 300,000 votes less than their rivals, winning 288 seats to the Conservatives' 260.

Snow, c. 1926. Scene between Buntingford and Cottered. Bert Thody with his dog Brenda, Ernie Smith (the bandleader), next to him. Will Smith and Charlie Worboys also there.

Dedication of War Memorial 11 Sept 1920. The Buntingford War Memorial was erected at the South end of the Market Hill in front of the Almshouses and St. Peter's. As well as the names of the men from Buntingford who were killed in the Great War it carries the initials (on another face) of C.L.F. – Claud Lovat Fraser – and it has been assumed that he designed the monument although there was no mention of this in contemporary reports of its unveiling: credit being given to a Bishop's Stortford firm. The cost was £170 raised by private subscription and the ceremony took place on Saturday evening, 11 September, 1920.

## Ten

# Buntingford at War

Ready for battle, 1914–18. Harry Jackson took this shot, and many more, of his fellow townsmen. 226 Buntingford men joined up; 44 did not return including three brothers to whom a memorial window was later placed in St. Richard's Church. Of 36 Aspenden servicemen, 10 were killed; Wyddial 27 and 6; Westmill 46 and 9.

2nd Battalion Bedfordshires 1914–1918. Some faces from other group photos – football, band, fire brigade – can be recognised here.

Scouts shrine, 23 May 1917. Scouts war shrine was designed and made by the Scoutmaster, C. Miles, also the Town's barber, as a tribute to the Boy Scouts who were serving in the Great War. By the date of the unveiling, 23rd May 1917, four had already been killed. Their names were in the centre panel and the names of the others were in the two outer ones. Major H.A. Anderson, President of the Troop, introduced Mrs. Pinckney, of Little Court, to unveil the memorial.

Scouts shrine: details. Thankfully, no further former scouts were lost.

Peace Celebrations, Little Court, 1919. Peace after the Great War was celebrated in Buntingford in June 1919. the photograph shows some 150 ex-service men grouped together at Little Court. Only two men are not wearing either a cap or a hat. There was a grand parade led by a Jazz Band and the Beckett Dramatic Company in fancy costume. At noon there was a united church service on the Market Hill followed by a hot dinner of roast beef, plum pudding, beer and minerals in a huge marquee at Little Court. Feeding started again at 4 p.m. when 300 children sat down to tea, followed at 5 p.m. by 400 women and then another meal for the men at 6. Each man received two ounces of tobacco. Then followed a sports programme, Country Dancing and fireworks as the finale.

Aspenden Peace Celebrations 19 June 1919. Aspenden folk celebrate peace on the village green. Behind can be seen Charles H. Poulton's workshop and house, The Apiary.

Tank in High Street, c. 1942. Only twenty years later the "war to end wars" was proved to have been no such thing. The tank is travelling south along the High Street past Moss's Wine Stores.

REME Depot 23 September 1943. A Royal Electrical and Mechanical Engineers depot was built at Hillside, opposite St. Francis' Convent, and many local women worked there alongside the REME soldiers. Tanks and other armoured vehicles were brought to Buntingford by rail and road. Here a tank is being sprayed after overhaul.

REME Depot 23 September 1943. Hilda Webb, nearest camera, Flo Smith and another local girl are dismantling motor cycle engines.

Land Army, c. 1943. Many girls joined the Womens' Land Army to help grow the food desperately needed for the country. This group were based at Wyddial Hall.

Buntingford platoon, Home Guard, c. 1943. Back row from left: Sam Hall, Albert Coxall, George Crouch, George Warner, George Scott, Frank Aylott, David Rout, Wybert Miles, Alec Postle. Middle row: Ron Deards, Jack Arbon, Walter Reed, Harry Mayes, Stan Thody, Clem Moule, George Attwood, Horace Mayes, Cyril Saunders. Front row: Bill Game, Augustus Harris, Fred Seymour, Limbury Roff, Charles Tyrwhitt-Drake, Stan Smith, Len Ward, Artie Dray, Jim Plumb.

Railway Home Guard, *c.* 1943. There was a special detachment for the railway commanded by the booking clerk with the station master as a private. Back row, from left: Bernard Ansell, -?-, -?-,Bernard Smith, -?-, Tom Sidney, Tom Gray. Sitting: Chris Bradley, Mr. Harvey (stationmaster), Stan Waters, Mervyn Corp, Mr Renshaw (stationmaster, Standon), Mr Martin, Alf Manhood. In front: Mr Aldridge, on left, and Harry Dobbs.

Officers of A Company, 1st Battalion Herts Home Guard. September 1944. Back from left: CQMS Harris, 2/Lts. S.F. Smith, E.R. Linnell, F.E. Winyard, J.C. Wilkerson, C.R. Turney, J.O. Norris, C. Reyersbach, C.S.M. Morris. Middle row: 2/Lts S.R. Pigg, S.C. Waters, C..A. Turney, M.C., Lts. L.G.J. Roff, W.M. Morris, R.H. Worboys, W.F. Sermons, N.J. Borman. E.S. Handley. Sitting: Lieut. M.E. Corp, Lieut .H.Field, Capt W.R.Kemsley, Major T.H. Veasey, M.C., Capt. A. Wigfield, M.O., Lieut. G.R. Watts, Lieut. A.G. Brant.

Evacuees Sept 1939. The North Hackney Central School for Girls was evacuated to the Buntingford area in September 1939. At first they were billetted in the villages around the town. Enid Pimm, Joan Beech and Joan Tagg were made welcome at Cromer Farm, Cromer.

Fifth Year at N. Hackney Central School, Buntingford, June 1942 The girls had their lessons at the newly opened Buntingford Secondary School. Petrol shortages meant that the girls had to be relocated in Buntingford itself in private houses and in a hostel, the Bowling Green. In the right hand group at the back from the left are Kathleen Wheeler (daughter of the headmaster of the Buntingford School). Enid Pimm, Jean White, and at the end Enid Muffett. Second from right in the front row is Joan Tagg.

Warships Week, 28 March 1942. To encourage national savings, various functions were held throughout the country. Large "thermometers" showed daily the running total. Warships Week was to raise £40,000 to "lift from the stocks" the mine-sweeping trawler Lady Philomena. The horses came from the Cox's Orange Pippin Orchards at Stonebury and they towed the disguised cart from the railway station to the top of the town and back to the Market Hill where the auction took place.

Warships Week, 28 March 1942. Many items, including livestock, were given for the auction. The purchaser received War Loan bonds for the total bid. Commander Swinley, of Longmead, was the Commander of a minesweeper, and he was the first auctioneer being succeeded by Captain Sanders of Cottered in top hat and disguised by a Spanish-style beard. Miss Joan Bowman noted the amounts bid.

*Above:* Nomads F.C. 1942–3. The war-time football team was known as the Nomads. It started playing at Hertford, then Westmill, Hillside, and then the Football Ground, Buntingford. Dr. Alan Wigfield was the president. Back row, from left: B.B.D. Aylott, G. Crouch, W. Smith, R. Emery, P.W. Plumb (treasurer). Middle row: J.Aldridge, R.Head, F.W.Aylott (secretary), A.Whitbread. Front: D.A. Jordan, R.C. Skipp (vice-capt), A.G. Warner (captain), A. Chambers, L. Poulton.

*Left:* Wings for Victory Week 5–12 June 1943. The week started with a fête and entertainments at the Senior School, then on Sunday a military and civil defence parade starting from Corneybury Park, proceeding to the station and returning to the Market Hill. During the week there was billiards, boxing, a whist drive, sports, two dances, a fun fair and the auction on the final day.

**BUNTINGFORD AND DISTRICT**
*Wings for Victory Week—*
**JUNE 5–12 1943**

OFFICIAL PROGRAMME
PRICE
**3**D.

# Eleven

# Round the District

Westmill, c. 1923. Frequently, with justice, described as the prettiest village in Hertfordshire, it is sited well off Ermine Street. It had its own historian in the early years of this century, Archibald Jackson, and his work forms the basis for Ewing's Westmill. Thomas T. Greg, who inherited Coles Park, was a considerable benefactor, building the village hall and also providing a museum which no longer exists (much of its contents are now in Stevenage Museum).

Westmill Church, c. 1920. St. Mary's has Anglo-Saxon work remaining in the SE angle of the nave and although the church was, like many others locally, heavily restored in the late nineteenth century, many other early features can be seen. Dr. Henry Pepys, a former rector, installed the east window in memory of his four children who are buried there.

Congregational Chapel, Sandon.

Congregational Chapel, Sandon, c. 1920. A scattered parish, Sandon consists of Ends and Greens. There were formerly two Congregational chapels and there are what has been suggested as the remains of the oldest windmill in the country.

Church End, Sandon, c. 1920. All Saints' Church is architecturally remarkable for the two large seventeenth-century buttresses supporting the tower.

Wallington Church, c. 1920 Wallington is somewhat remote from Buntingford but was in the Buntingford Rural District and also in the poor law union. George Orwell lived here, intermittently, from 1936 to 1940.

Rushden Church, *c.* 1920. Like Sandon, Rushden has its Greens and Ends and is very scattered. The large mansion of Julians was largely rebuilt in 1937–39.

Braughing, *c.* 1942. Photographed during the Second World War, this picture formed part of a collection extolling the virtues of the English countryside. Braughing was an important centre during Roman times and the Romano-British cemetery excavations have yielded much of importance.

Hare Street, c. 1912. Two miles east of Buntingford, Hare Street developed along the road branching off Ermine Street at Puckeridge and leading to Cambridge. The hamlet is in three parishes, Layston, Little Hormead and Great Hormead.

Hare Street House, c. 1927. The facade is of Georgian brick but the house is much older and was bought by Robert Hugh Benson in 1907. He created a chapel from an old brew-house which stood at the back and is reached from the Hare Street to Hormead road.

The Church, Anstey, c. 1930. A small village four miles north-east of Buntingford, there are three noteworthy historical features: St. George's Norman church, the lychgate and the site of Anstey Castle, a large motte and bailey surrounded by a moat. There is a persistent legend about an ancient, devil-haunted subterranean passage between here and Cave Gate, about a mile distant.

Chipping Bridge, c. 1910. In the parish of Buckland, this hamlet was originally established as a market on Ermine Street, just over a mile north of Buntingford. The Royal Oak public house no longer exists and the mission room and Congregational chapel are now private residences.

The Goose Inn, Moor Green, *c.* 1912. Ardeley, some five miles west of Buntingford, has a Gardener's End, a Parker's Green, Munches Green and Moor Green where this long-forgotten hostelry stood.

Fire at St. Edmund's College, Sunday 29 July 1907. The Roman Catholic School and Seminary at Old Hall Green, five miles south of Buntingford, suffered a disastrous fire in which a third of the College was destroyed. Five brigades attended and Buntingford's is the jet on the left.

Japanese Garden, Cottered, c. 1937. Herbert Goode, a wealthy glass and china merchant, created the Japanese Garden between 1905 and 1926 by shipping many items from Japan and employing Japanese gardeners to maintain it. It fell into dubious ownership some years ago and police action was necessary to prevent the ornaments and other valuable objects from being dispersed. Its restoration is eagerly awaited.

St. John the Baptist Church, Cottered, c. 1900. This large village church has an impressive Medieval wall-painting of St. Christopher. The nave is aisleless and lofty. There are many fine houses in the village including Lordship House dating partly from the fifteenth century.